101
QUESTIONS & ANSWERS

WHO? WHAT?   WHERE? WHY?

Cars, Planes, Ships and Trains

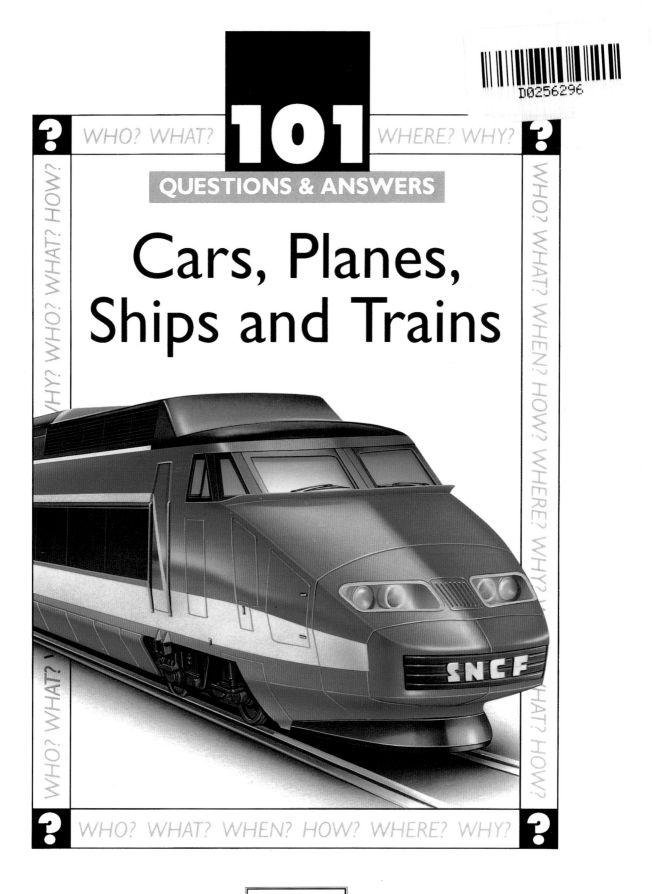

WHO? WHAT? WHEN? HOW? WHERE? WHY?

HAMLYN

GLOSSARY

articulated Refers to a type of lorry with two sections connected by a flexible joint.

atom A very small particle, the smallest part of a chemical element that takes part in a chemical reaction. Atoms are about a tenth of a millionth of a millimetre across.

battery A device that changes chemical energy into electricity.

catamaran A boat with two hulls connected by a deck above the water.

clutch Part of a drive system that transmits the engine power to the wheels. The power can be disconnected from the wheels by pressing the clutch pedal or pulling the clutch lever.

crankshaft The main rod, or shaft, inside an engine. The spinning crankshaft is linked by gears to the wheels and makes them spin too.

drag The force that tries to slow down a vehicle. It is caused by the air or water in contact with the vehicle's surfaces.

exhaust Waste gases from burning fuel in an engine.

force Something that makes an object move or change its direction of motion. Examples are gravity and magnetism.

fuel A material like coal, wood, gas or oil that is burned to release the chemical energy stored inside it.

gears Interlocking toothed wheels that reduce the high speed of an engine to the lower speed of the vehicle's wheels.

generator A machine that converts movement into electrical energy.

hydrofoil A ship that can increase its speed by lifting its hull out of the water on underwater wings, reducing drag.

jet engine A type of engine used in most large aircraft in which hot gases produced by burning fuel are expelled from the rear, pushing the vehicle forward.

lift The force that acts on wings or rotor blades to help an aircraft take off from the ground and keeps it in the air.

maglev Short for magnetic levitation, which is the use of forces that push magnets apart to lift objects off the ground or off a track.

orbit The circular or oval path of an object as it travels around a star or planet.

rocket An engine like a jet engine which works in space because it carries its own oxygen needed to burn the fuel.

rotor On a helicopter, a set of blades rotating around a central hub.

shuttle A type of vehicle that travels to and fro many times, usually along the same track or flightpath.

solar panels Devices, usually made from materials called semiconductors, that can convert the energy of sunlight into electrical energy.

submersible A craft designed to operate underwater for short periods.

thrust The force that makes a vehicle move, used especially in connection with rockets and aircraft jet engines.

valve A device that controls the flow of fuel and air inside an engine. One set of valves opens to let fuel and air into the engine and, when the fuel has been burned, a second set of valves opens to let the exhaust gases out.

First published in Great Britain in 1994 by
Hamlyn Children's Books
an imprint of Reed Children's Books Limited
Michelin House, 81 Fulham Road, London SW3 6RB,
and Auckland, Melbourne, Singapore and Toronto.

Copyright © Reed International Books Limited 1994

Designed and produced by Lionheart Books, London.

ISBN 0 600 583279 (HB)
ISBN 0 600 583848 (PB)

Printed in Belgium by Proost

British Library Cataloguing-in-Publication Data. A catalogue record for this book is available from the British Library.

Acknowledgements
Designer: Ben White
Editor: Lionel Bender
Media Conversion and Typesetting: Peter MacDonald
Project Editor: Veronica Pennycook.

Artwork credits
The Maltings Partnership: 4-9, 20-23, 28-29, 30-31(top). Russell and Russell Associates-Andrew McGuiness: 10-11. Hayward Art Group: 12-19, 24-25, 26-27(bottom), 35(top), 38(inset), 40, 41(top). Mark Bergin: 25(right), 26-27(top), 29(bottom), 30-31(bottom), 32-33, 34, 35(bottom), 36-37. Mike Saunders: 46-47. Janos Marffy: 38-39, 42-43, 44-45.

CONTENTS

This book contains question and answers on the following topics:

Ian Graham

How does a car work?

A car moves when its engine releases energy to turn the car's wheels. That energy, which is locked up in the fuel, is released as fuel is burned inside the engine. To go faster the driver presses the car's accelerator pedal. Two other pedals operate the brakes and the clutch, which is used for changing gear. The gears convert the rapid rotation of the engine output shaft to the slower rotation of the shafts that turn the wheels. Pressing the clutch pedal disconnects the engine from the gears.

WHY USE PETROL?
Petrol is the fuel most commonly used by cars because it burns very easily when it is mixed with air. This means that it also gives up the energy stored inside it very easily, enabling the car to start and move off promptly.

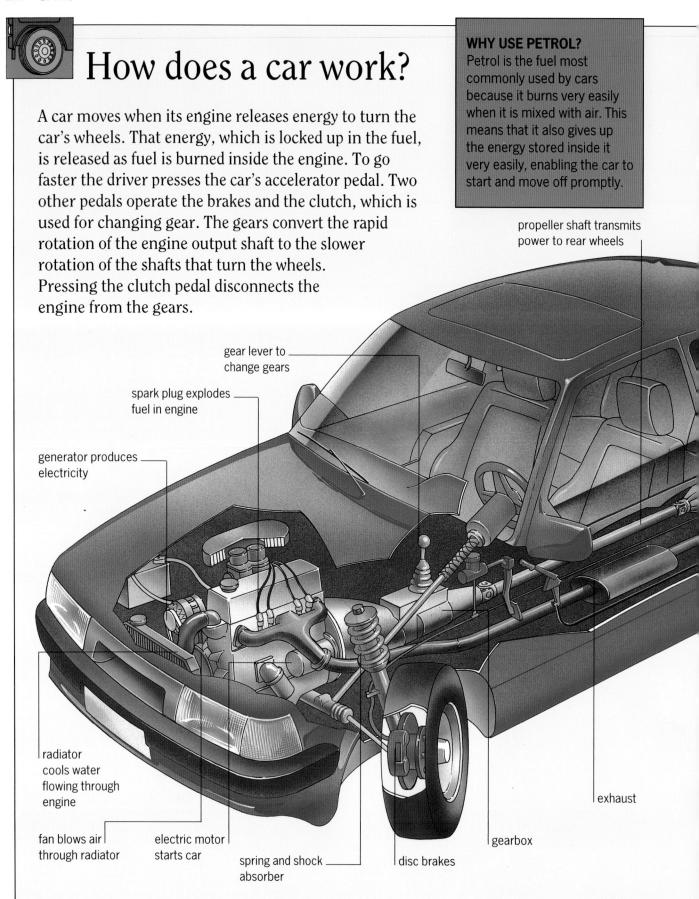

propeller shaft transmits power to rear wheels

gear lever to change gears

spark plug explodes fuel in engine

generator produces electricity

radiator cools water flowing through engine

fan blows air through radiator

electric motor starts car

spring and shock absorber

disc brakes

gearbox

exhaust

HOW TO STEER?

A car's steering wheel is linked to the front wheels by gears and levers, so that the steering wheel needs to be turned a long way for the car wheels to turn a little. This difference makes it easier to turn the steering wheel.

fuel tank

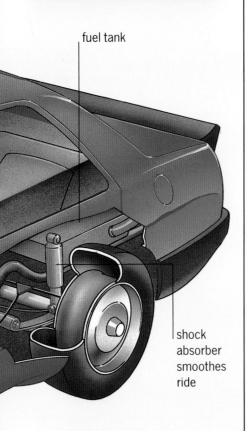

shock absorber smoothes ride

HOW TO STOP?

Brakes stop a car by changing its movement energy into other energy forms, mainly heat. Applying the brake forces oil through pipes to the brakes, where the oil presses pads against a metal disc (or drum) fixed to each wheel. Friction between them heats the disc and slows the car.

Can batteries power a van or truck?

Some vehicles are powered by electricity instead of by burning a fuel. The wheels are turned by an electric motor supplied with electricity from batteries. Electric vehicles are quieter than petrol-driven vehicles but they cannot travel as far without refuelling (recharging).

electric storage batteries

electric motor

air intake to cool motor

HOW TO REFUEL?

A petrol-driven car is refuelled by pouring more petrol into the fuel tank at a fuel station. To "refuel" an electric vehicle, the batteries are recharged (filled up with more electrical energy) by plugging them into an electrical supply. There are several ways to increase the vehicle's range. For example, the vehicle may be made from ultra-lightweight materials so that less energy is needed to move it. Also, when it brakes to slow down or stop, the unwanted movement energy can be used to drive a charging unit that generates extra electricity.

What happens inside a car engine?

A mixture of petrol and air is sucked into a cylinder by a piston that slides down inside the cylinder (1). The piston rises up, squeezing the mixture (2). A spark ignites the mixture, which expands and forces the piston down the cylinder (3).

The piston rises again and pushes the waste gases out (4). This is called the four-stroke cycle. Cars need at least four cylinders to produce the continuous power strokes that create an uninterrupted power output.

1 exhaust valve closed
inlet valve open
piston descends sucking in mixture

2 inlet valve closed
piston ascends compressing mixture

3 spark plug
ignited mixture forces piston down

4 exhaust gases forced out

Is a motorcycle engine like a car's?

The four-cylinder, four-stroke car engine is too big for many motorcycles. They use a smaller and simpler engine that produces power on every second movement (stroke) of the piston. It is called a two-stroke engine. The fins attached to the outside of the engine help to carry heat away from the cylinder. They provide an extra-large surface area that is cooled by air rushing through the engine as the motorcycle moves along.

piston

spark plug

fins

crankshaft

What is a catalytic converter?

Fitted to the engine, a catalytic converter makes poisonous engine fumes safe. Inside the converter, a honeycomb coated with metals such as platinum causes chemical reactions in the fumes, changing them into harmless gases like nitrogen and water vapour.

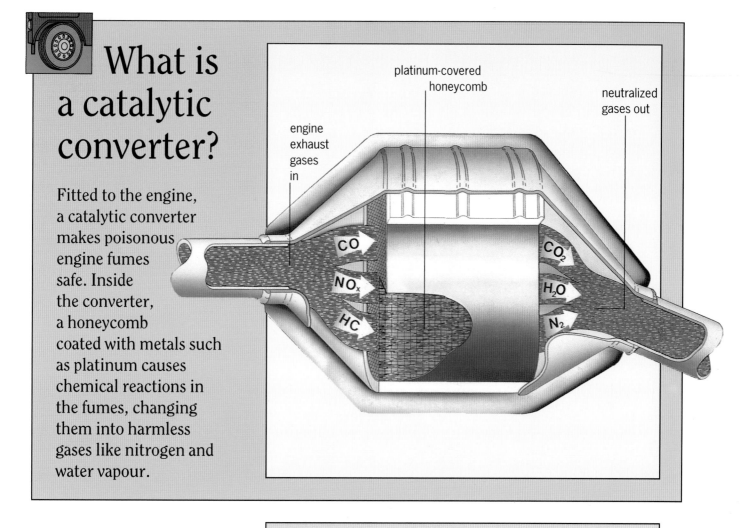

platinum-covered honeycomb

neutralized gases out

engine exhaust gases in

CO

NO_x

HC

CO_2

H_2O

N_2

A rising piston (1) compresses the fuel mixture, which is ignited by a spark. The piston falls (2), sucking in more fuel mixture and pushing out the burned fuel.

HOW MANY CYLINDERS?
A two-stroke motorcycle engine may have one, two, three or four cyclinders. Engines with more than one cylinder vibrate less than single-cylinder engines and so they are more comfortable to ride. The largest motorcycles have four-stroke engines similar to car engines.

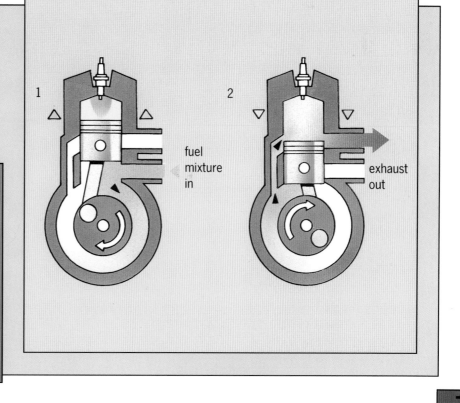

1

2

fuel mixture in

exhaust out

How do motorcycles balance?

The first motorcycles, built in the 1860s, were powered by a steam engine behind the saddle. This arrangement made the bike top-heavy and liable to topple over. By 1901, the modern design had been adopted, with the heavy engine mounted low down in the middle of the frame.

electric start button

throttle

front brake lever

fuel tank

battery

The power of the engine is transferred to the rear wheel by a chain or a belt. The fuel is stored in a tank above the engine in front of the rider. The rider's weight over the rear wheel helps to press the rear tyre against the ground and increase its grip. To steer a motorcycle, the rider uses the handlebars and leans over with the bike when going into a bend.

rear suspension

rear brake pedal

exhaust

engine

piston

HOW TO STOP?
Like cars, motorbikes are slowed and stopped by disc brakes. Braking forces pads to grip the discs fixed to the wheels. The discs have holes drilled in them to reduce weight and to allow air to circulate and cool them.

WHAT ARE THE CONTROLS?
The front brake and the clutch are operated by squeezing levers at the ends of the handlebars. Twisting the right-hand grip speeds up the engine. Two pedals, one on either side, change gear and apply the rear brake.

HOW FAST DO THEY GO?
In motorcycle racing on tracks, riders often reach speeds of more than 200 km/h. The fastest racing bikes can exceed 300 km/h. The world speed record for a motorcycle stands at 513 km/h, set in 1978.

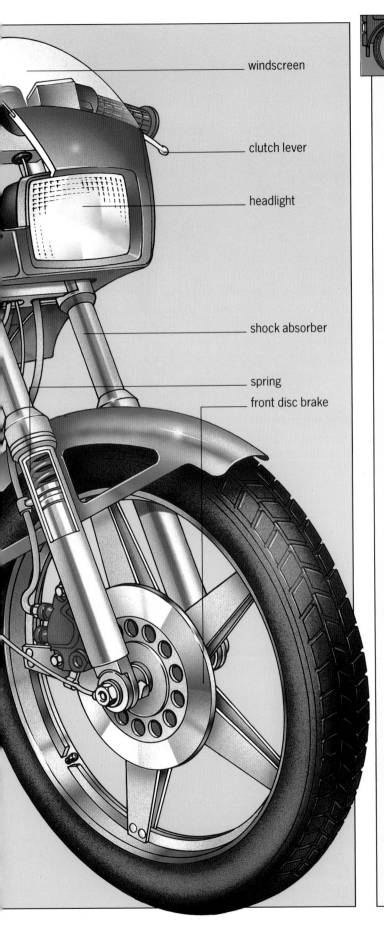

- windscreen
- clutch lever
- headlight
- shock absorber
- spring
- front disc brake

How tough are rubber tyres?

Tyres are very tough indeed. Underneath the rubber tread and sidewalls, there are several layers, called plies, made from fabric strengthened with steel wire. The tread allows any water that is under the tyre to drain away.

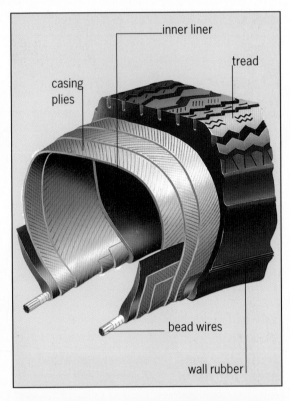

- inner liner
- tread
- casing plies
- bead wires
- wall rubber

DO ALL TYRES HAVE INNER TUBES?
Bicycle tyres have an inflatable and airtight inner tube inside the tyre to hold in the air. Car tyres used to have inner tubes too, but modern car tyres are tubeless. As the tyre is inflated, it forms an airtight seal with the wheel rim. It can support 50 times its own weight.

How do diesel-electric trains work?

The modern diesel-electric locomotive is an electric train that carries its own power plant for making electricity. Its main advantage is that it does not need any overhead power-supply wires or a power rail alongside the track. The train's diesel engines do not drive the wheels directly. Instead, their job is to power a generator which makes electricity. The electricity is supplied to electric motors which turn the locomotive's wheels.

HOW DOES STEAM PULL TRAINS?

The first trains were powered by steam, made by burning coal to heat water. The steam was used to force pistons up and down cylinders which, through a system of levers and cranks, turned the wheels.

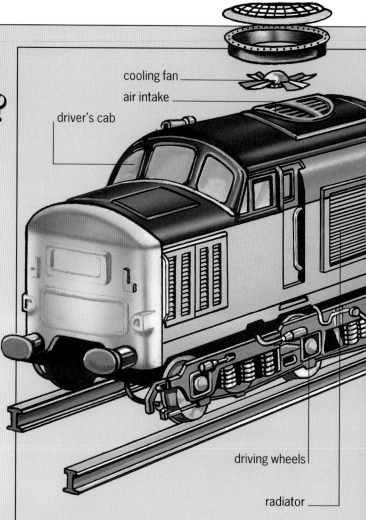

cooling fan

air intake

driver's cab

driving wheels

radiator

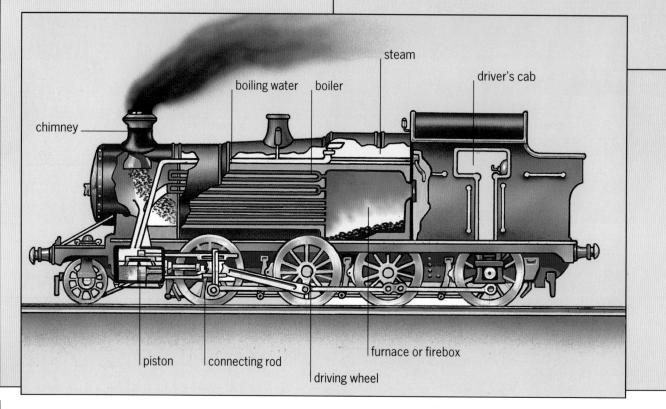

chimney

boiling water

boiler

steam

driver's cab

piston

connecting rod

driving wheel

furnace or firebox

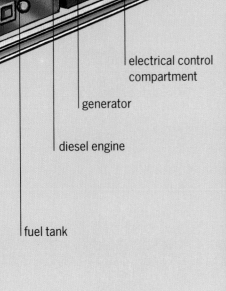

electrical control
compartment

generator

diesel engine

fuel tank

What is the Channel shuttle?

Railway services beneath the English Channel are due to begin in 1994. Special shuttle trains will make the 50-km journey through the Channel Tunnel in 35 minutes. A passenger shuttle will pull 26 wagons carrying 185 cars. Freight shuttles will pull 25 wagons each carrying a 44-tonne truck. An electric locomotive will be coupled to each end of the train.

WHICH TRAINS FLY?

The magnetic levitation train, or maglev for short, floats above its special track on an invisible magnetic cushion. Magnetic fields propel the train along as it moves above the track. Since the train does not touch the track, there is no friction to hold it back. Maglevs can therefore travel extremely fast. Experimental maglevs in Germany and Japan have reached speeds of more than 400 km/h.

HOW BIG ARE TRAINS?

The longest ever passenger train was recorded in Belgium in 1991. Made up of 70 coaches pulled by a single electric locomotive, it moved along the track for 1.7 km. The longest and heaviest freight train known, in South Africa in 1989, consisted of 660 freight wagons carrying almost 70,000 tonnes. More than 7 km in length, it was pulled by nine electric and seven diesel-electric locomotives.

How fast can trains go?

The first passenger trains travelled at 40-50 km/h. In Japan today, the famous Bullet trains reach top speeds of 210 km/h. The fastest passenger train currently in service is the French TGV (*Train à Grande Vitesse*). It has a top speed of 290 km/h and often averages more than 220 km/h.

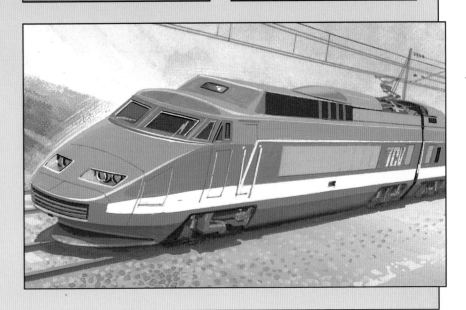

When is a truck articulated?

Trucks are either straight or articulated. In a straight truck, the driver's cab, engine and load platform are all built on the same rigid chassis (frame). An articulated truck has a separate tractor unit (the driver's cab and engine) and load platform. The two are linked by a rotating joint that allows the truck to bend in the middle. Articulated trucks are easier to manœuvre. They also allow the driver to disconnect the tractor unit from one load and link it up with another so that the tractor unit is not standing idle while a truck is being loaded or unloaded.

driver's cab

exhaust stack

diesel engine

fuel tank

trailer

How do trolley-buses work?

Trolleybuses are buses powered by electric motors supplied with electricity from overhead wires. On the first models, the power was collected by a trolley running on top of the wires. Later, two long poles linked the bus to the wires.

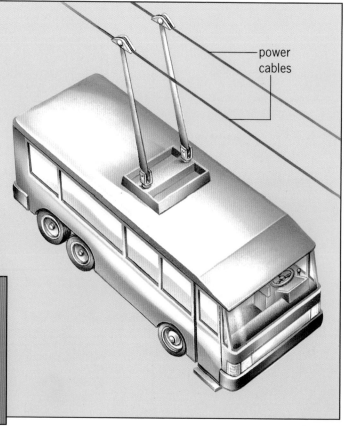

power cables

HOW OLD ARE TROLLEYBUSES?
The first trolleybuses entered service in the 19th century. They were spacious, fast and quiet compared to the steam-buses of the day. In some parts of Europe, they ran until the 1950s. By then, petrol-driven buses were cheaper to run and could do so without overhead wires.

Can a tram come off the rails?

Trams run on steel wheels rolling on steel rails laid in the road surface. The wheels are specially shaped to prevent the tram from sliding sideways and falling off the track. Like train wheels, they have a shoulder or "flange" standing out from the inside edge which stops any sideways movement. Flanged wheels date from the 17th century, when wooden wagons ran on wooden rails.

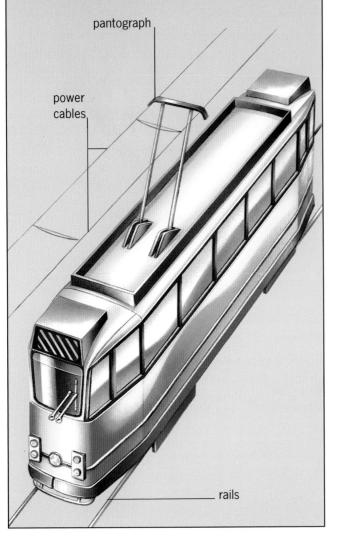

pantograph

power cables

rails

How do caterpillar tracks work?

Some vehicles are so heavy that if they were to run on ordinary wheels over soft ground they would sink in. One solution is to spread the vehicle's weight over a larger area by replacing the wheels with a pair of flexible belts. These are called caterpillar tracks and are usually made from a chain of flat metal links. A tracked vehicle is steered by slowing down or stopping the caterpillar track on one side.

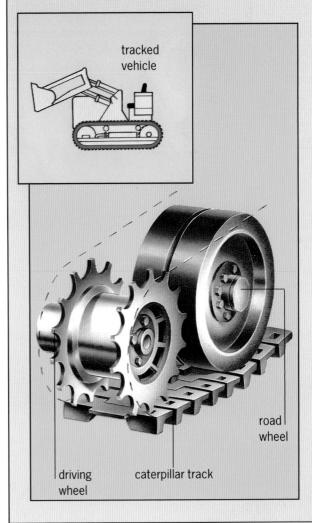

tracked vehicle

driving wheel

caterpillar track

road wheel

Why do ships float?

Ships are mostly built from steel, a material that is much heavier than water. If you throw a piece of metal into water, a coin for example, it sinks. So why does a ship not sink? The reason is that the steel that the ship is made of is in the form of a thin sheet bent up to form a steep-sided hull. Shaped like this, the ship can displace (push aside) its own weight of water and avoid falling so low that the water washes over the top and sinks it. In other words, the ship weighs the same as the water it displaces and it therefore stops sinking and floats.

WHAT SORT OF ENGINES?

Most ships are powered by diesel engines, which are reliable, cheap to run and easy to repair. Some fast military ships have gas turbines similar to jet aircraft engines. The jet exhaust from the engine spins a turbine which turns the ship's propeller. A few ships are nuclear-powered. They use a nuclear reactor to heat water and make steam. The steam spins a turbine which turns the propeller.

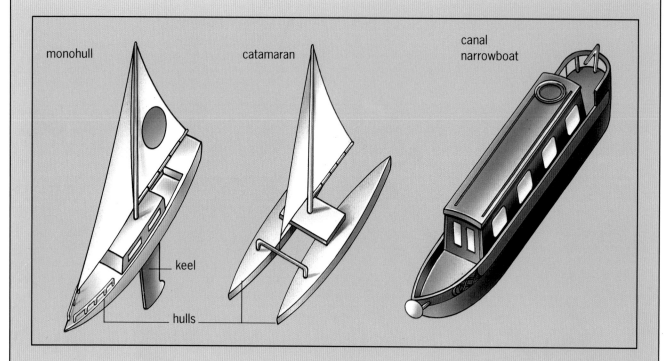

monohull

catamaran

canal narrowboat

keel

hulls

WHAT IS THE LARGEST?

The biggest ships afloat today are VLCCs, Very Large Crude Carriers. These oil tankers can weigh up to half a million tonnes when fully loaded with crude (unrefined) oil. They are so big, more than 350 m long, that the crew sometimes use bicycles to get around the deck.

HOW DO SHIPS STOP?

Ships cannot apply brakes as a car or truck does. Even if a ship stops its engines, it will continue moving through the water, slowing down very gradually. It can halt more quickly by spinning its propellers in reverse. The largest ships take hundreds of metres to stop.

WHO FIRST MADE SHIPS?

People have used rafts and dugout canoes since prehistoric times. The ancient Egyptians were making large ships from bundles of reeds up to 8,000 years ago. By 4,000 years ago, the Minoan people on Crete had developed large wooden sailing ships.

What is the Plimsoll mark?

How deep a ship lies in the water depends on the weight of its load and the kind of water. The Plimsoll mark shows how heavily the ship can be loaded in safety. Different letter codes stand for Tropical Freshwater, Freshwater, Tropical Saltwater, Summer Saltwater, Winter Saltwater and Winter in the North Atlantic.

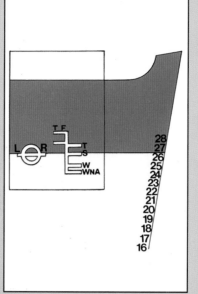

WHO WAS PLIMSOLL?

Before the Plimsoll mark was introduced, old ships were often overloaded and insured for more than they were worth. When they sank, the owners collected all the insurance money. Samuel Plimsoll was the Member of Parliament for Derby who helped to introduce the Merchant Shipping Act of 1876. This required all cargo ships to have a safe load line – a circle with a line through it – which soon became known as the Plimsoll mark. For stamping out "coffin-ships" as they were known, Plimsoll was called the sailors' friend.

How do yachts sail into the wind?

The first sailing ships could only sail in the same direction as the wind. Then, about 2,000 years ago, Arab sailors invented a sail that enabled ships to sail in every direction except directly into the wind. Nowadays, yachts can sail into the wind using a lateen sail, which is set at an angle to the wind.

wind sucks sail forwards and to one side

yacht moves forwards through water

WHAT IS RIGGING?

The ropes and wires that hold up a yacht's mast and operate the sails are called the rigging. Standing rigging holds the mast up while running rigging raises and lowers the sails.

WHAT IS A KEEL FOR?

The keel is the lowest part of a yacht's hull. The force of water pressing on it helps stop the yacht from being pushed sideways and off course when the wind blows against the sails.

Why do some ships have two hulls?

As a ship sails along, water rubbing against its hull creates a force, called drag, that tries to slow it down. One way of reducing drag is to reduce the area of hull in contact with the water. This can be done by having two or more long thin hulls instead of one fat one. A multi-hulled craft also has more deck and storage space, and its great width makes it difficult to capsize (overturn).

HOW OLD ARE THEY?
Multi-hulled boats have been used by Pacific islanders for thousands of years. In the 17th century, Europeans started copying them. Our word catamaran comes from a Tamil (South Indian) word meaning tied wood. The Pacific catamarans had one main hull with one or two smaller "outriggers" at the side to stop the boat from being blown over.

How do ships use water jets?

Some ships are powered by water jets instead of propellers. Jet engines suck water in from the sea and pump it out of the stern (the back of the ship) at high speed. By varying the force of the jets on each side of the ship, they can also be used to steer the vessel.

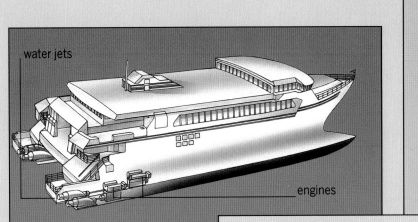

water jets

engines

DID YOU KNOW . . .

● A 1,500-tonne twin-hulled ferry, the *Castalia*, was built as long ago as 1874 for the Dover–Calais route across the English Channel?

● The winner of the first recorded race in the open sea, in the 17th century, was a twin-hulled boat called *Experiment*?

● The winner of the first Round Britain and Ireland Race in 1966 was a trimaran (with three hulls) called *Toria*?

● By carefully shaping the tunnels between the hulls of a trimaran or quadrimaran (four hulls), wind pressure in the tunnels can be made to raise the hulls and boost the craft's speed?

● A monohull is less likely to capsize in rough seas than a multi-hull because of its heavy keel?

HOW BIG IS THE BIGGEST CATAMARAN?

The world's biggest catamaran is the 74-m-long SeaCat. In 1990 it made the fastest crossing of the Atlantic ocean by a passenger craft, taking three days, seven hours and 55 minutes. It can carry up to 450 passengers and 80 cars across the English Channel in as little as 35 minutes.

What is a ro-ro?

One of the most familiar sights at a busy modern port is a ship whose massive bow or stern doors open up to reveal a vast loading deck inside. This is a roll-on roll-off ferry, to give it its full name, or ro-ro, for short. The ro-ro is specially built to transport road vehicles quickly and conveniently on short sea voyages. Cars, coaches and trucks drive on board through doors at one end of the ship and out again through doors at the other end to disembark when the ship docks.

HOW OLD IS THE RO-RO?
Cars used to be loaded onto ships by cranes, which lowered them into the ship's hold. When international trade and tourism increased after 1945, a faster loading method was needed. During World War II, soldiers and tanks were often transported from ship to shore by landing craft with bow doors that lowered to form a ramp. The idea was later adapted and became the ro-ro.

HOW BIG ARE THEY?

The ro-ro has been so successful that ferry operators have ordered larger and larger ships for busy routes such as the English Channel. The biggest on record is the *Silja Serenade*. This 58,000-tonne giant is 203 m long and 31 m across its beam (widest point). It carries up to 450 cars and 2,500 passengers between Helsinki, Finland, and Travemunde in Germany.

How is cargo carried?

Goods sent by sea used to be transported in crates, sacks and boxes of all shapes and sizes. It was left to the loaders, called stevedores, to decide how to achieve the maximum safe load in the ship's hold. Then, in the 1960s, the container ship was developed. Nowadays, when cargo arrives at the port it is already packed in standard containers. These are loaded quickly by special cranes into container-sized cells in the ship, so that no space is wasted.

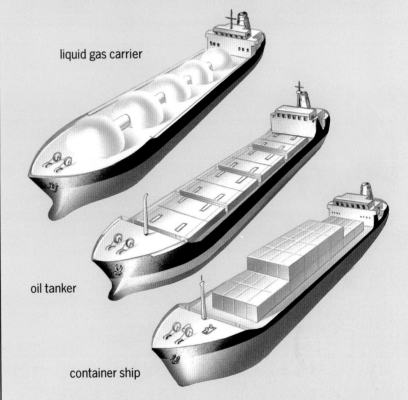

liquid gas carrier

oil tanker

container ship

WHAT DO TUGS DO?

The largest ships are built for the open sea. Once in harbour, it is much safer to use tugs to manoeuvre them into and out of their berths. Tugs are small but very powerful boats capable of towing or pushing much larger ships.

ARE SHIPS LIKE CARS?

Yes. The largest and busiest ports have traffic control systems monitored by radar. Controllers watch the movements of all the ships on radar screens and communicate with them by radio. Ships must keep to the correct sea lanes.

How do atoms power a submarine?

Atoms release enormous amounts of energy when they split apart. Uranium atoms split very easily, sending out particles that make nearby uranium atoms split too. The energy released heats water to make steam and the steam drives turbines that turn the propeller.

periscopes

conning tower

torpedoes in racks

torpedo tubes

control and periscope rooms

bunks

What is a submersible?

An underwater craft that can only work with the help of a ship is called a submersible. The ship carries it out to sea for launching. On resurfacing at the end of its dive, the submersible is taken on board the ship again.

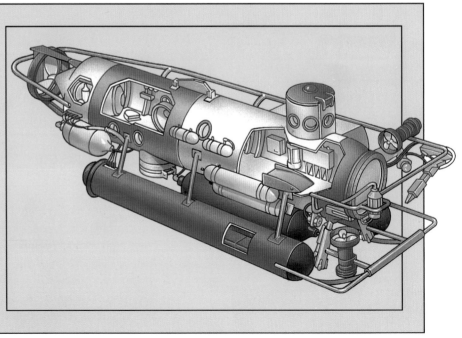

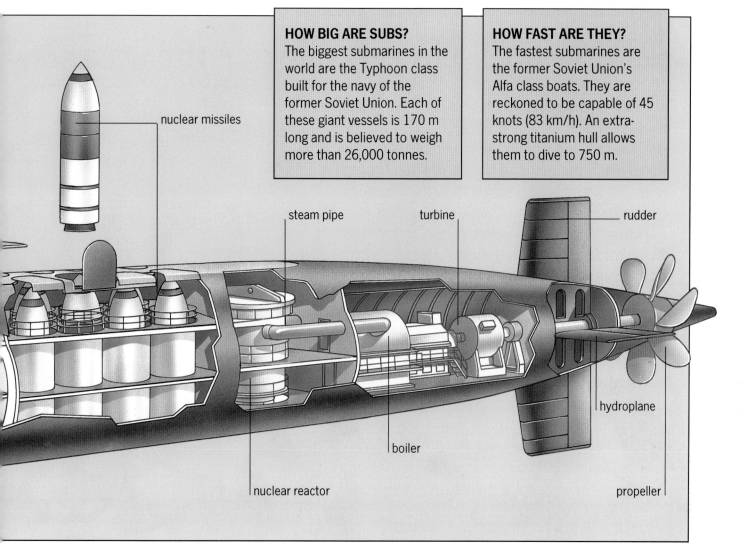

nuclear missiles

HOW BIG ARE SUBS?
The biggest submarines in the world are the Typhoon class built for the navy of the former Soviet Union. Each of these giant vessels is 170 m long and is believed to weigh more than 26,000 tonnes.

HOW FAST ARE THEY?
The fastest submarines are the former Soviet Union's Alfa class boats. They are reckoned to be capable of 45 knots (83 km/h). An extra-strong titanium hull allows them to dive to 750 m.

steam pipe

turbine

rudder

boiler

nuclear reactor

hydroplane

propeller

How do submarines sink?

To sink below the surface a submarine opens the valves in its hull, letting seawater flood into the empty ballast tanks. The submarine becomes heavier than water and sinks. To make it surface again, the water is forced out of the tanks by compressed air.

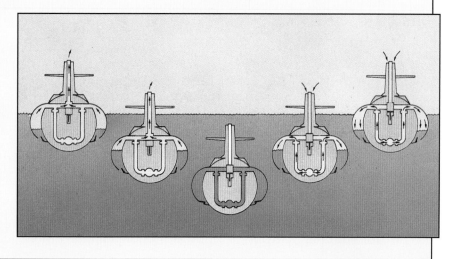

How does a hovercraft ride the waves?

If a ship could somehow raise its hull out of the water, it could reduce the effect of water dragging on the hull and slowing the ship down. One possibility is to blow air underneath the vessel so powerfully that the hull is completely pushed up out of the water. Drag is eliminated and the whole craft glides along effortlessly on a cushion of air. The hovercraft uses this method. It can fly over land or sea equally easily. Vehicles that work in this way are also called air-cushion vehicles.

People were experimenting with air under ships as long ago as the 1870s. In the 1950s, the British inventor Sir Christopher Cockerell finally solved the problem of how to keep the air cushion in place. The result was the hovercraft. Today, the largest hovercraft, SRN4, weighs 300 tonnes and can carry 400 passengers and 60 cars.

radio antenna

radar antenna

control deck

front loading door

passenger compartment

WHAT IS A HYDROFOIL?

A boat that reduces drag on its hull by using wing-shaped foils to raise the hull out of the water is called a hydrofoil. It is the foils that provide the necessary lifting force. Surface-piercing foils (left) are popular in passenger-carrying hydrofoils. Submerged foils (right) are better in rough seas because their angle is adjustable.

passenger boat hydrofoil

hydrofoil for rough sea

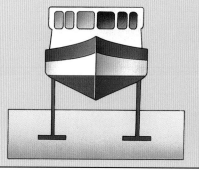

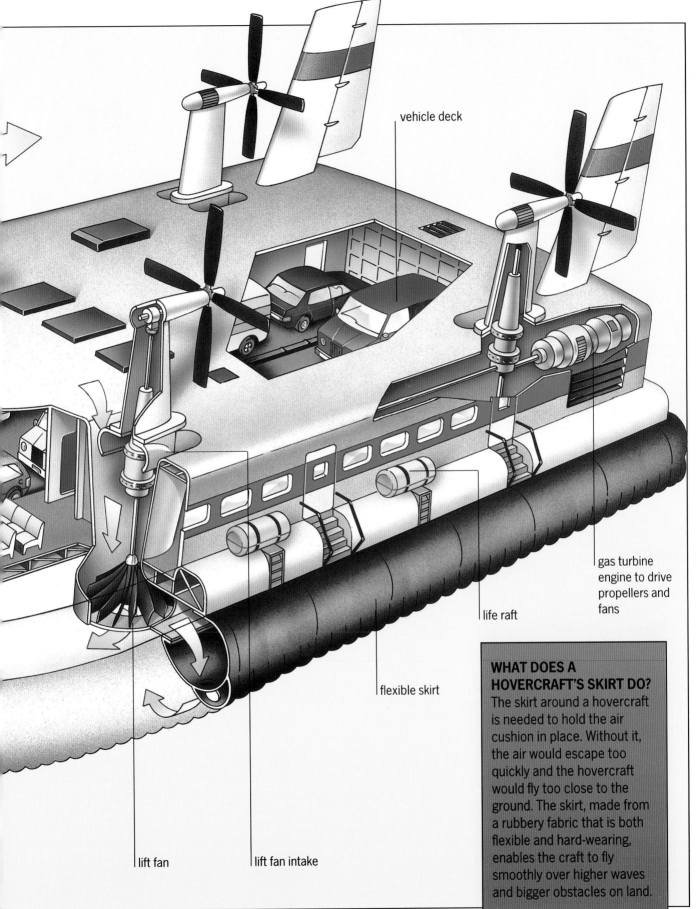

vehicle deck

gas turbine
engine to drive
propellers and
fans

life raft

flexible skirt

lift fan

lift fan intake

**WHAT DOES A
HOVERCRAFT'S SKIRT DO?**
The skirt around a hovercraft
is needed to hold the air
cushion in place. Without it,
the air would escape too
quickly and the hovercraft
would fly too close to the
ground. The skirt, made from
a rubbery fabric that is both
flexible and hard-wearing,
enables the craft to fly
smoothly over higher waves
and bigger obstacles on land.

How is a plane steered?

A plane's wings and tail are fitted with hinged panels called control surfaces. These are linked to the controls in the cockpit. When the pilot operates the controls, one or more of the panels pivots out from the wing or tail. Air pushing against a panel deflects that part of the plane in the opposite direction. There are five control surfaces.

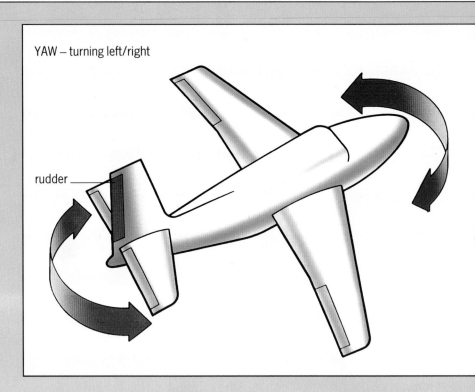

YAW – turning left/right

rudder

Swivelling the rudder out to the left pushes the plane's tail to the right, making the plane's nose turn left. Similarly, to turn the plane to the right the rudder is also turned to the right, forcing the tail round to the left. This turning motion is known as yaw.

Why are planes different shapes?

An aeroplane's shape determines its maximum speed. Low-speed planes have wings at right angles to the fuselage (body). Faster subsonic airliners have swept-back wings. The supersonic airliner Concorde has wings swept back to form a delta shape. Swing-wing jets are designed to fly at a wide range of speeds.

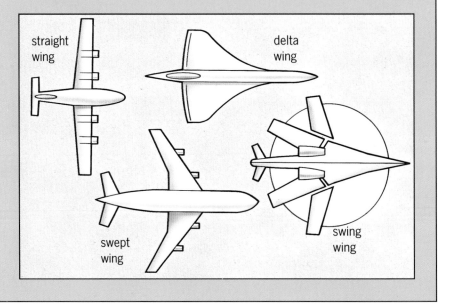

straight wing

delta wing

swept wing

swing wing

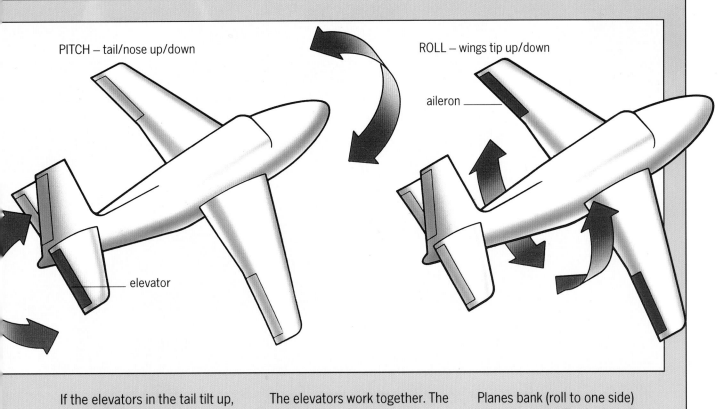

PITCH – tail/nose up/down

elevator

ROLL – wings tip up/down

aileron

If the elevators in the tail tilt up, the tail is pushed down and the plane climbs. If they tilt down, it dives. This is called pitch.

The elevators work together. The ailerons in the wings work in opposition. When one is up and one is down the plane rolls.

Planes bank (roll to one side) when they turn. To do this, the pilot has to operate the rudder and the ailerons together.

When is a plane a boat?

The flying boat is in fact a plane that can take off and land on water. Flying boats were popular in the 1920s and 1930s, when there were fewer airports.

They provided passenger services between seaports and lakes. Flying boats are still used in countries such as Canada where there are huge lakes to land on.

Flying boat

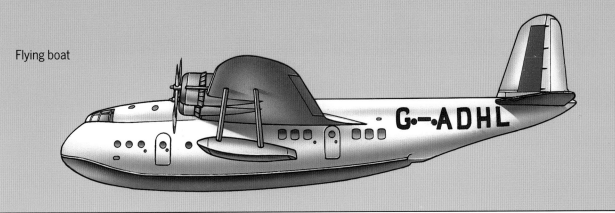

G-ADHL

Do all planes have two wings?

The first warplanes that flew in World War I (1914–1918) were biplanes, with two pairs of wings, or triplanes, with three pairs. Both these designs were popular because the wings and their wooden struts and bracing wires formed a very strong structure. As flying speeds increased, the struts and wires were found to produce too much air resistance and slowed the planes down.

How do wings create lift?

Wings can lift a heavy aircraft into the air because of their shape. When a plane moves forwards at speed, the curved top of the wing forces the air above the wing to flow farther and faster than the air below it. This reduces the air pressure above the wing, sucking it upwards.

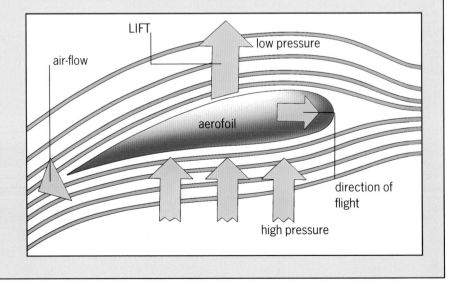

LIFT

low pressure

air-flow

aerofoil

direction of flight

high pressure

To overcome this problem, plane-makers began to make more streamlined monoplanes, with one pair of wings. The wings were stiffened from the inside by rigid metal tubes. When World War II started in 1939, monoplanes were already taking over.

WHAT IS A DOGFIGHT?
When the first warplanes fought each other in World War I, their twisting manœuvres and the noise of the engines and machine-gun fire suggested a vicious fight between two dogs. These aerial combats became known as dogfights. Today, jet fighter pilots are still schooled in how to overcome enemy aircraft in modern dogfights.

When do wings not work?

Wings only work when air flows smoothly over them. If the smooth air-flow breaks up, the air pressure above the wing ceases to be less than it is below the wing.

The suction force that holds the aircraft up in the air is destroyed. This happens if the wing is tilted up too much. The wing and the aircraft are said to have stalled.

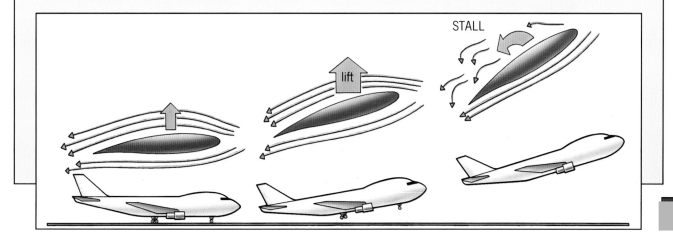

STALL

lift

How do helicopters fly?

Aeroplane wings create lift only when the aircraft is moving forwards at great speed. Helicopters, without having to rush along a runway, create enough lift to take off by spinning their rotor blades.

How do rotor blades work?

Rotor blades act like long thin wings. As they whirl round above the helicopter, they cut through the air and create lift. The pilot can change the amount of lift by operating a control that tilts the blades. Tilting the leading edge up increases the lift.

How is it steered?

When the lift created by the rotor blades exceeds the helicopter's weight, the craft rises (1). If the disc traced out by the tips of the rotor blades is tilted down at the front, the down-draught is angled backwards, pushing the craft forwards (2). Tilting the disc down at the back has the opposite effect (3). To hover, the lift must equal the helicopter's weight (4).

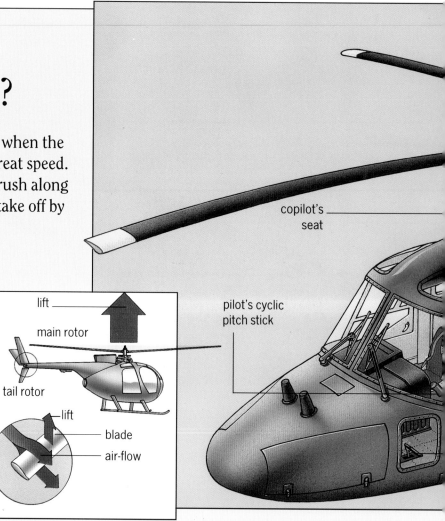

copilot's seat

pilot's cyclic pitch stick

lift

main rotor

tail rotor

lift

blade

air-flow

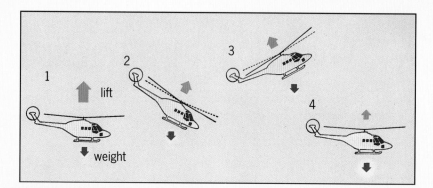

1

lift

weight

2

3

4

HOW DOES IT TURN?

A small rotor at the end of the tail boom stops the helicopter from spinning in the opposite direction to the main rotor. Varying its thrust allows the helicopter to turn.

HOW FAST CAN IT GO?

On 11th August 1986, a Westland Lynx set a world air speed record for helicopters at 400.87 km/h. The rotor blade tips approached the speed of sound.

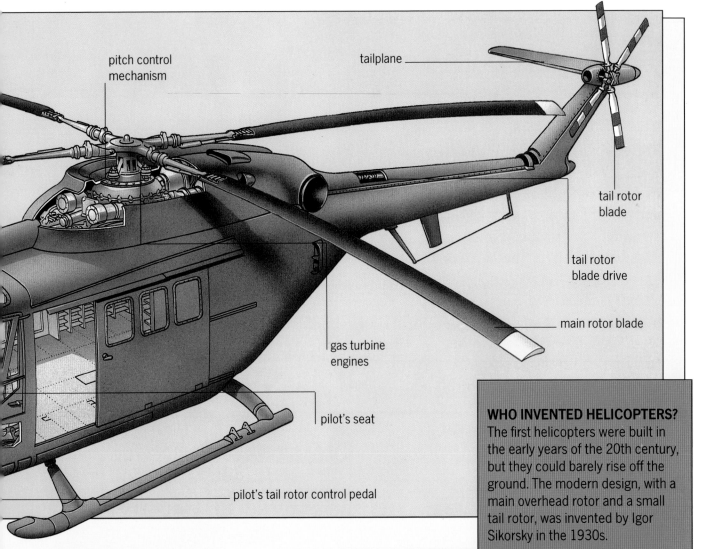

pitch control mechanism

tailplane

tail rotor blade

tail rotor blade drive

main rotor blade

gas turbine engines

pilot's seat

pilot's tail rotor control pedal

WHO INVENTED HELICOPTERS?
The first helicopters were built in the early years of the 20th century, but they could barely rise off the ground. The modern design, with a main overhead rotor and a small tail rotor, was invented by Igor Sikorsky in the 1930s.

Who uses helicopters?

Helicopters are ideal for transporting people and equipment to or from areas where aeroplanes cannot land. Rescue helicopters can hover over people in danger on a mountain or in the sea and winch them up to safety. They can also pluck injured sailors from ships at sea and fly them to hospital, or take offshore workers to and from their oil or gas rigs.

Which is the biggest airliner?

The world's largest passenger plane is the Boeing 747. This giant jet aircraft made its first test flight on 9th February 1969, and carried its first fare-paying passengers on a flight across the Atlantic Ocean on 21st January 1970. The 747 soon became known as the "Jumbo Jet" because of its size. It is 70 m long, measures 60 m across from wing-tip to wing-tip and, at 19 m high, towers over all other passenger aircraft. Its passenger cabin can carry up to 624 people, 69 of them seated in an upper passenger deck behind the flight deck. A freight version of the aircraft is also in service.

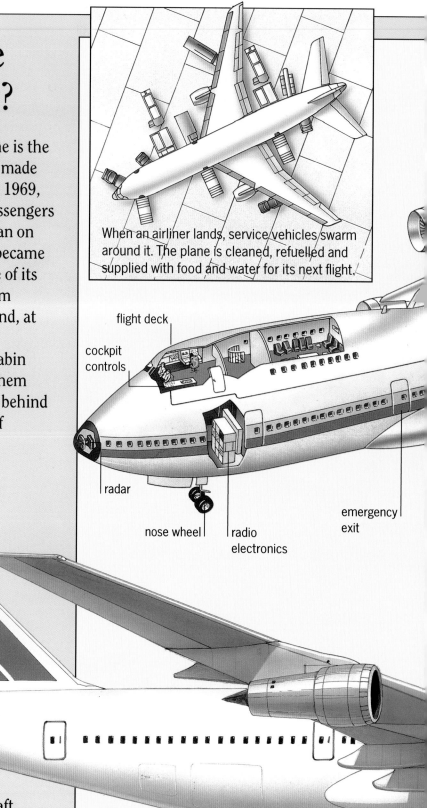

When an airliner lands, service vehicles swarm around it. The plane is cleaned, refuelled and supplied with food and water for its next flight.

flight deck

cockpit controls

radar

nose wheel

radio electronics

emergency exit

Each of a Boeing 747 Jumbo Jet's four engines pushes the aircraft along with a force of more than 25 tonnes. Together, the engines burn 13,500 litres of fuel, weighing 11 tonnes, every hour.

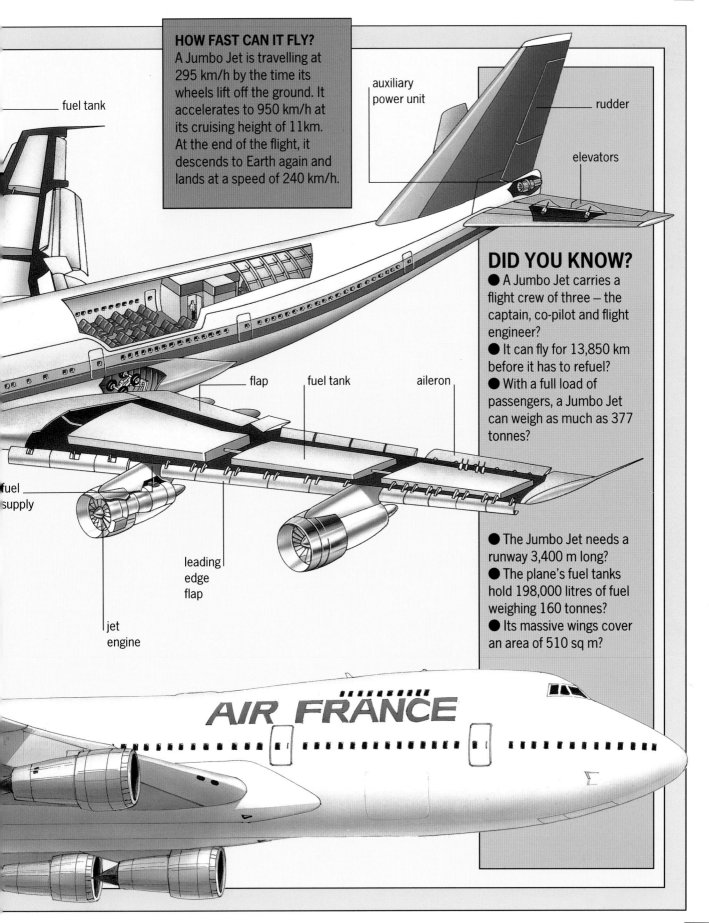

HOW FAST CAN IT FLY?
A Jumbo Jet is travelling at 295 km/h by the time its wheels lift off the ground. It accelerates to 950 km/h at its cruising height of 11km. At the end of the flight, it descends to Earth again and lands at a speed of 240 km/h.

fuel tank

auxiliary power unit

rudder

elevators

DID YOU KNOW?
● A Jumbo Jet carries a flight crew of three — the captain, co-pilot and flight engineer?
● It can fly for 13,850 km before it has to refuel?
● With a full load of passengers, a Jumbo Jet can weigh as much as 377 tonnes?

● The Jumbo Jet needs a runway 3,400 m long?
● The plane's fuel tanks hold 198,000 litres of fuel weighing 160 tonnes?
● Its massive wings cover an area of 510 sq m?

flap

fuel tank

aileron

fuel supply

leading edge flap

jet engine

AIR FRANCE

What were the first aircraft?

The first flying machines were probably kites made in China about 3,000 years ago. When the kite was held at an angle to the wind, air pushing against it lifted it up. Some of these kites could lift a person into the air, as here.

Did kites lead to aeroplanes?

The Wright Brothers, who made the first aeroplane flight in 1903, spent four years learning how to control kites and gliders before attempting powered flight. The American showman Samuel Cody built people-carrying kites in the early 1900s and developed them into gliders. He also made the first powered flight in Britain.

DID YOU KNOW . . .
● The German aviation pioneer Otto Lilienthal made 2,000 glider flights between 1893 and 1896 before he was killed when his glider crashed?
● The Wright Brothers tossed a coin to decide who would make the world's first aeroplane flight?
● Wilbur won, but the plane stuck in the sand at the end of its take-off run and failed to take off?
● His brother Orville took the next turn and made the historic flight?
● The first aeroplane flight lasted for only 12 seconds?
● The brothers made three more flights, the longest (by Wilbur) lasting 59 seconds and covering 260 m?
● The world's first successful aeroplane was called *Flyer I*? It was a biplane (two pairs of wings) with a wing-span of 12.3 m?

WHO WAS BLÉRIOT?
The first international aeroplane flight was made between France and England in 1909. The pilot was Louis Blériot, a French car engineer. The aircraft was a *Blériot XI* monoplane, the pilot's own design, with a wing-span of 7.8 m and a top speed of 75 km/h. Blériot took off from Les Boraques, near Calais, and landed again 37 minutes later on a grassy hill beside Dover Castle in Kent. The historic flight earned him a prize of £1,000, awarded by the London *Daily Mail* newspaper. Blériot's success helped to establish the basic design of the modern monoplane.

How do gliders fly?

The best technology often copies something that has already developed naturally in the animal or plant kingdom. Birds that spend a lot of their time gliding, such as the albatross, have long thin wings to extract the greatest lift from the wind. Glider wings are also long and thin to reduce air resistance and maximize lift.

HOW FAR CAN THEY FLY?

Most glider pilots land at the same airfield they have taken off from. However, in the right conditions, and with an expert pilot, gliders can travel huge distances. In 1972, Hans-Werner Grosse flew an ASK-12 glider from Lübeck in Germany to Biarritz in France, a distance of 1,460 km.

HOW DO THEY TAKE OFF?

Most gliders cannot take off by themselves. They have to be towed at the end of a cable pulled by a powered aeroplane. After the towing plane and the glider are both in the air, the glider pilot operates a catch which drops the towing cable. Some gliders have a small lightweight engine and propeller that enable them to take off under their own power. Once the glider is airborne, the engine is folded away into the fuselage. It can be pulled out again to help keep the glider aloft in poor soaring conditions.

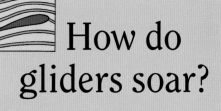

How do gliders soar?

An unpowered aircraft like a glider does not plunge to the ground when it is released from its towing plane. It can soar higher if the pilot can find rising columns of warm air, called thermals. They are caused by hot spots on the ground. Birds also use thermals, so they can often be found by watching birds circling nearby.

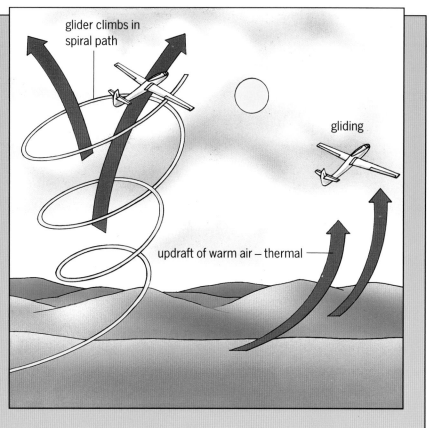

glider climbs in spiral path

gliding

updraft of warm air – thermal

How do skydivers fly?

Skydivers may look as if they are flying, but they are really falling in a controlled way. By holding their arms and legs in certain positions, they can steer themselves around quite precisely. They can even link up and join hands. In 1992, a record-breaking 150 skydivers held hands in the air over Belgium. To land safely, they release a parachute from a sack on their back. The parachute fills with air and creates enough resistance to slow the parachutist down to a safe landing speed.

escaping air

drag

weight

35

How can airships be lighter than air?

An airship is a large structure made from materials that are heavier than air. It seems impossible, then, for it to be able to float up into the sky. However, the skin of the craft is a huge envelope filled with helium gas, and helium is lighter than air. In fact, there is so much helium inside the airship that it makes the whole craft lighter than air. The modern airship is powered by piston engines driving ducted propellers – aeroplane propellers inside ducts (tubes). The craft is steered by control surfaces in the same way as an aircraft.

DID YOU KNOW...

● The airship was invented in 1852 by Henri Giffard, who hung a steam engine under a long thin balloon and added a rudder to steer it?

● In the 1930s, huge airships regularly carried passengers across the Atlantic Ocean?

● Also in the 1930s, the US Navy airships *Akron* (below) and *Macon* were fitted with hooks to carry fighter planes?

● The largest airship ever built was the German *Graf Zeppelin II*, 245 m long and weighing 213 tonnes?

WHAT ARE BLIMPS?
Modern airships are semi-rigid. The envelope is stretched over a stiff metal frame. In the past, some airships had no frame. The gas pressure inside them kept them in shape. They were called blimps.

WHAT IS A GONDOLA?
The crew and passengers sit in a cabin, called a gondola, slung underneath the envelope. The gondola is fixed to the airship's frame. The modern airship Skyship 600 has a crew of two and carries 13 passengers.

HOW FAST ARE AIRSHIPS?
The first airship, built by Henri Giffard, could manage about 10 km/h. The 245-m-long *Hindenburg*, completed in 1936, was capable of carrying 75 passengers across the Atlantic Ocean in luxurious conditions at 131 km/h.

How do balloons rise?

Like an airship, a balloon rises into the sky because it is lighter than air. Although there are some helium-filled gas balloons, most balloons now use hot air to create lift. Hot air is lighter than cold air and so it rises. The balloon traps the hot air and is carried up into the sky with it. Gas burners slung underneath the balloon can be turned on and off as necessary to heat the air and control the balloon's height. The pilot and passengers travel in a basket hanging underneath the balloon. Gas for the burners is stored in high-pressure cylinders carried in the basket.

WHO WAS FIRST?
The first balloon was test-flown by a sheep, a dog and a cockerel in France in 1783. The balloon was built by the Montgolfier brothers. Later the same year, Pilâtre de Rozier and the Marquis d'Arlandes became the first human balloonists.

HOW TO BEGIN?
A balloon arrives at its launch-site folded up in a bag. Once it is unpacked, the neck is held open and some air is blown inside. A flame directed at the open neck heats the air. The balloon soon floats upwards and fills with air.

HOW TO LAND?
If the pilot stops using the burner, the air in the balloon soon cools down and the balloon begins to descend. An experienced balloonist can use the burner to control the balloon's descent and make a safe "soft" landing.

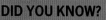

How do rockets work?

Fuel will not burn without oxygen. On Earth, engines use oxygen in the air to burn their fuel, but there is no oxygen in space so rockets have to carry their own supply. The fuel and oxygen, stored under pressure in separate tanks, are pumped into a combustion chamber where they are mixed and burned. The burning gas expands and rushes out of the engine nozzle, propelling the rocket in the opposite direction to that of the gas.

DID YOU KNOW?
● Solid fuel rockets similar to modern fireworks were being used by the Chinese as weapons of war by the 11th century?
● The German V-2 rocket was the first supersonic guided missile and was used as a powerful weapon in World War II?
● The most powerful rocket is the *Energiya* launcher developed by the former Soviet Union, with a thrust of 3,480 tonnes?

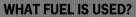

WHAT FUEL IS USED?
Liquid hydrogen is a common rocket fuel. Hydrogen is normally a gas, but at −235°C it changes to a liquid, which takes up less space.

What are rocket stages?

Modern rockets are actually several (usually three) separate rockets stacked on top of one another. These are called stages. As each stage uses up its fuel, it is dropped from the rest of the rocket and the next stage fires. The use of rocket stages saves the engines energy that would be wasted in carrying empty fuel tanks.

1 First stage engines
2 First stage
3 Interstage link
4 Second stage engines
5 Second stage
6 Third stage engines

HOW ARE THEY STEERED?
Rockets are steered by making their engine nozzles swivel to change the direction of the thrust caused by the exhaust.

WHERE TO LAUNCH FROM?
Launch sites are usually located near the Equator. This is because the Earth's spin is at its fastest there and so gives the rocket an extra "kick" to help it on its way. US rockets take off from Cape Canaveral (Florida). European rockets are launched from Kourou (French Guiana) while Russian rockets are fired from Tyuratam (Kazakhstan).

How are satellites launched into space?

The Ariane rocket can place two satellites in orbit. Boosters that help launch the rocket soon burn out and fall away (1), followed by the first stage. The cover around the satellites is discarded (2). The second stage burns out (3) and the third stage fires. The first satellite is ejected by springs (4), followed by the second (5). Their solar panels unfold and supply them with electricity. The third stage is boosted to prevent it colliding with the satellites (6).

WHEN WAS THE FIRST?
The first satellite to be placed in orbit around the Earth was Sputnik 1, launched by the former Soviet Union on 4th October 1957. The 58-cm metal sphere weighing 84 kg carried a radio transmitter. Its signals were received on Earth for 21 days before its batteries ran out of power.

WHAT ARE SPACE PROBES?
Most spacecraft orbit the Earth, but some, called space probes, explore the planets. Some space probes fly so far from the Sun that they have to use nuclear power plants instead of solar panels to make electricity.

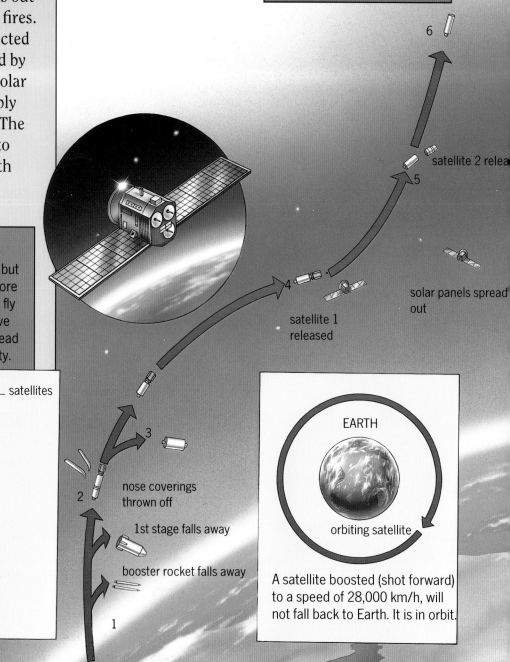

6

satellite 2 relea

5

solar panels spread out

4

satellite 1 released

3

2 nose coverings thrown off

1st stage falls away

booster rocket falls away

1

EARTH

orbiting satellite

A satellite boosted (shot forward) to a speed of 28,000 km/h, will not fall back to Earth. It is in orbit.

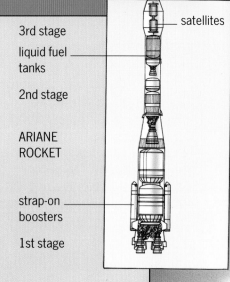

3rd stage

satellites

liquid fuel tanks

2nd stage

ARIANE ROCKET

strap-on boosters

1st stage

How high can a satellite be?

Space officially begins 100 km above the Earth's surface. Satellites orbit the Earth at much greater heights so that the atmosphere cannot drag them down. The first satellite, Sputnik 1, was placed in an orbit whose height ranged from 228 km to 947 km. Most satellites are at between 200 km and 1,000 km. Some specialist satellites, like those used for navigation, orbit the Earth as high as 20,000 km. The most distant satellites are comsats (communications satellites), which are in orbit at a height of 36,000 km.

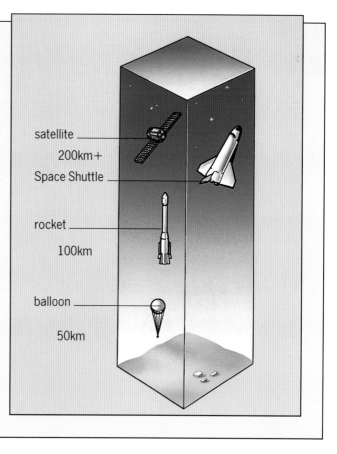

satellite
200km+
Space Shuttle

rocket
100km

balloon
50km

What are orbits?

The path followed by a satellite around a planet is called an orbit. There are different types of orbit. A communications satellite orbits high above the Equator, keeping pace with the Earth and hanging over the same spot on the surface. A spy satellite, orbiting from pole to pole, "sees" different parts of the Earth spinning below. The type of orbit depends on the satellite's function.

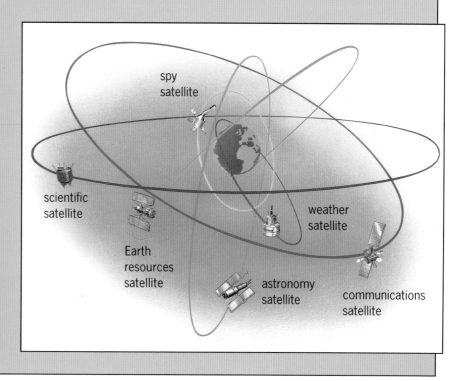

spy satellite

scientific satellite

Earth resources satellite

weather satellite

astronomy satellite

communications satellite

How big are manned spacecraft?

The weight and size of a spacecraft is limited by the power of its launch rocket. The first US manned spacecraft, Mercury, was very small and weighed only about 1.4 tonnes. More powerful rockets made bigger spacecraft possible. The Apollo spacecraft that carried astronauts to the Moon weighed 45 tonnes. The Space Shuttle (see page 46) orbiter in use today weighs 80 tonnes. The Mercury capsule was just big enough for one astronaut to squeeze into a seat. The Space Shuttle is much more roomy, with 71 cubic metres of crew space spread over three decks.

MERCURY
The first US manned spacecraft was a tiny capsule that stood only 2.9 m high and measured 1.89 m across its base. There were eight Mercury flights between 1961 and 1963. The longest lasted 34 hours 20 minutes.

SOYUZ
Soyuz spacecraft were used in the former Soviet Union from the 1960s. Updated versions still ferry crews and supplies to the *Mir* space station. Soyuz carries a crew of three and has solar panels for electrical power.

YURI GAGARIN
The Soviet major was the first person in space in April 1961.

APOLLO

The Apollo spacecraft that landed the first people on the Moon was a tiny cone-shaped module only 3.5 m from nose to heat shield. Linked to it was a cylindrical service module that provided oxygen, power and an engine.

JOHN GLENN

In 1962, Glenn was the first American to orbit the Earth.

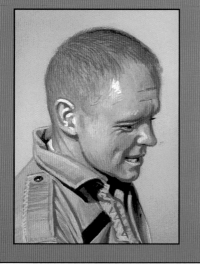

WHAT IS RE-ENTRY?

Before a spacecraft can return to Earth from space, it has to re-enter the atmosphere. As it plunges into the atmosphere, air rubbing against it makes it very hot. A heat shield absorbs the intense heat and prevents the craft from burning up.

How did astronauts reach the Moon?

On 16th July 1969, Apollo 11 blasted off from Cape Canaveral with Neil Armstrong, Edwin "Buzz" Aldrin and Michael Collins on board. Three days later they were in lunar orbit. Armstrong and Aldrin landed the lunar module on the Moon while Collins stayed in the command module. They all returned to Earth on 24th July.

HOW BIG WAS THE ROCKET?
The Saturn V rocket that launched the Apollo spacecraft to the Moon stood 111 m high, three times the height of the first manned rocket launchers such as Vostok.

Vostok   Saturn V

What was the *Eagle*?

The Apollo 11 lunar module was called *Eagle*. On 20th July 1969, when Neil Armstrong sent a radio message to Earth saying, "The Eagle has landed", it meant that he and Edwin "Buzz" Aldrin had become the first people to land on the Moon.

When was a car driven on the Moon?

The last three Apollo flights (Apollos 15–17) took a battery-powered car to the Moon so that the astronauts could explore a wider area. It weighed 209 kg, but could carry 490 kg. A family car carries only half its own weight. The load included two astronauts and up to 127 kg of rock samples, tools and communications equipment.

What is an MMU?

Astronauts have been leaving their spacecraft and "spacewalking" since 1965. But they were always attached to the spacecraft by a safety line. The first person to float completely free of his spacecraft and become a satellite of the Earth was US Space Shuttle astronaut Bruce McCandless in 1984. He strapped on a gas-jet backpack called MMU (Manned Manœuvring Unit) and flew around outside on his own.

HOW IS IT FLOWN?
The MMU is propelled by 24 nitrogen gas jets fired by controllers at the ends of its armrests. It has an autopilot system that can keep the astronaut in the same position automatically.

How is the Space Shuttle launched?

The Space Shuttle is the first reusable spacecraft. It takes off from a launch pad at Cape Canaveral in Florida, USA. During lift-off, its rocket engines are supplied with fuel by an external fuel tank. When the tank is nearly empty, it falls back to Earth. A pair of rocket boosters help to provide enough thrust (force) to lift the craft into the air. The boosters too fall back to Earth when their job is done.

HOW FAST DOES IT FLY?
By the time the Shuttle's Orbiter (spaceplane) leaves the atmosphere and enters orbit around the Earth, it is travelling at 28,000 km/h.

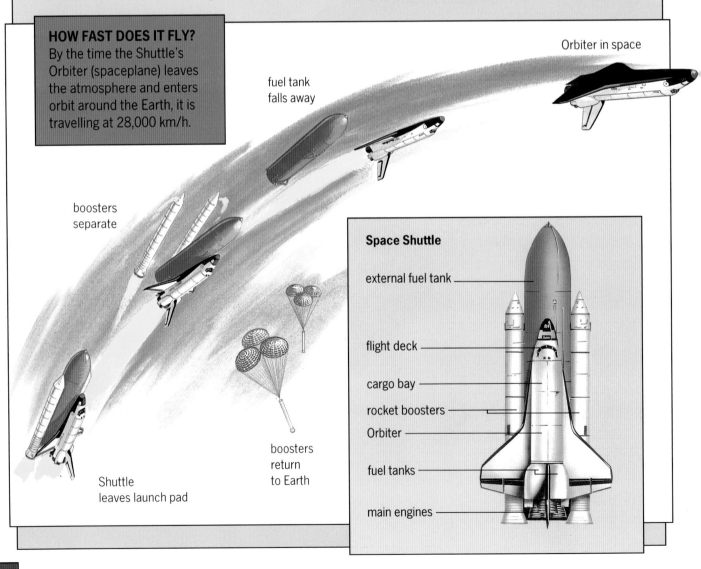

Orbiter in space

fuel tank falls away

boosters separate

boosters return to Earth

Shuttle leaves launch pad

Space Shuttle

external fuel tank

flight deck

cargo bay

rocket boosters

Orbiter

fuel tanks

main engines

How does the Orbiter land?

The Orbiter can carry a crew of seven astronauts on a space flight lasting up to 30 days. During that time the crew may have launched satellites from the 18-m-long payload bay and carried out many scientific experiments. At the end of the mission, rocket thrusters slow the craft down and it begins to re-enter the atmosphere. It glides down and lands like an unpowered aircraft on a runway.

Orbiter re-enters Earth's atmosphere

HOW MANY ORBITERS?
There have been six Orbiters. *Enterprise* made test flights in the atmosphere. *Columbia* was the first to fly into space in 1981. *Challenger* followed in 1983. *Discovery* first flew in 1984, *Atlantis* in 1985, and *Endeavor* in 1993.

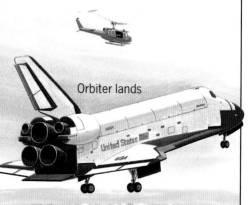

Orbiter lands

HOW HOT DOES IT GET?
The leading edges of the Orbiter's wings are heated to 2,700°C during re-entry into the atmosphere. Even the coolest part of the craft, the top of the fuselage, reaches 600°C. It is protected by special tiles that stop the heat from reaching the metal skin.

INDEX